A Wartime scrapbook

Chris S. Stephens

pont
library

Contents

FIVE INCHES!

Wartime Scraps

The Second World War affected the lives of all our families – parents, grandparents and, in some cases, great-grandparents of those who are reading this book today. There was fighting right across the world, on land, on sea and in the air – and its effects reached into every home, in every corner of Wales. It was the most widespread and, some say, the most destructive war in history. Every reader will know something about it.

We know how children were evacuated from the big cities, each with a brown label fastened to a coat button and a gas mask slung around their necks.

We know that food was rationed, and shoppers with empty baskets joined the end of a queue, not knowing what they were queuing for until they reached the front.

We know all about the comic escapades in *Dad's Army*, and the bombers in the Blitz, and that carrots are supposed to help you see in the dark – to spot a German spy at fifty paces.

These and other scraps of knowledge appear on every page of this book, reminding us perhaps of the Victorian scrapbooks which the writer Thackeray mentioned as early as 1854: then, as now, such books were full 'of comic prints of grandpapa's time'. To us, the photographs and pictures may seem 'comic' at times, and yet they show us just what life was like for those who lived as children and adults in the 1940s.

Evacuees

Even before the war actually started, children began to be moved out of industrial areas and cities, for their own safety. From September 1st 1939, railway stations became sad places, as children carrying gas masks, small suitcases and favourite toys said goodbye to their parents, not sure when they would see them again. About one and a half million children were sent away from English cities. Many came to Wales. Sometimes whole schools came together, sometimes just families.

Wartime friends: Jano Bevan, on her mother's knee (left) and her older brothers and sister spent happy times with Marjorie, Stan and Joyce, who had been evacuated to Llysyfran from London.

We were actually evacuated to Hastings first, on the south coast of England, but after Dunkirk they said it was too dangerous, so we came to Wales. It was a bit of a culture shock! In Hastings we'd been in a doctor's house, with a butler and a housemaid . . . we arrived at Clarbeston Road station at 2 in the morning . . . we were last to find a place, as I'd promised my mother we wouldn't be split up – the 'baby' needed us to stay together . . . Jano's mother wanted two girls really . . . but we stayed together.

I remember I woke up that first morning between two enormous men; there wasn't a bed for me, you see, and I'd been put in the bed that the two older brothers of the house shared. – Marjorie, Stan and Violet Ledger

Life in the country was strange, but to some it was the happiest time of their lives. Some evacuees still visit the places where they spent their childhood, and meet up with old friends.

Fifty years on, Jano meets up with Marjorie, Stan and their older sister, Violet, who was evacuated to Ammanford.

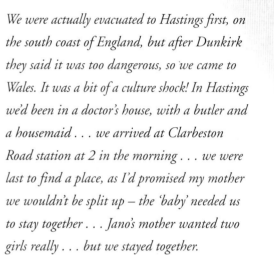

Advice on how to look after evacuees in Caernarfonshire.

Cyngor Dosbarth Gwledig Gwyr

At y Teuluoedd a'r Personau a gymerant i mewn Ffoaduriaid ar adeg o argyfwng

CYFARWYDDIADAU A DARPARIADAU.

City children found the country life very different – but a pony called 'Bessy', and a chance for rides to the village in the trap, made being an evacuee an adventure for the Ledger children. (April 1941)

From a poem by Jenny Sullivan With thanks to the late, great Ernie Morgan

When the evacuees came to Raglan our boys and theirs walked round each other, sniffing like dogs, suspicious, their hackles raised, snarling a bit.
This was our place, this was.
What were these townies doing down by here?
Didn't belong, did they?

They had daps, some of them, not hobnails like us farm kids.
They didn't know one end of a cow from the other, and we used to ambush one like Red Indians and shove him in a field with a cow. We'd tell him 'It's a bull!'
And shout, 'Run, evacuee kid, run!'
And laugh to see him panic.

Of course there are two sides to the stories. Country children, particularly in the remote areas of North Wales, often found their visitors very unusual.

'We had two Jewish boys, twins, and their mother . . . A Housing Officer came with them . . . and there were already ten of us in the house: six children, my parents, a man servant and a maid servant . . . and the mother, she was very particular. On Saturdays she'd ask my mother for the brass candlesticks and a tablecloth, and be praying for some time . . . When they went to bed each night, she'd demand a hot bath for the boys, in a house where there was only well water and a pump! Now we'd never seen anything like her; she wore plunging necklines, and false eyelashes.

When evacuees first arrived there was often trouble, as you might imagine – especially in the village schools – as children got to know one another.

Carrie's War

'Oh it'll be such fun,' their mother had said when she kissed them goodbye at the station. 'Living in the country instead of the stuffy old city. You'll love it, you see if you don't!' As if Hitler had arranged this old war for their benefit, just so that Carrie and Nick could be sent away in a train with gas masks slung over their shoulders and their names on cards round their necks. Labelled like parcels – Caroline Wendy Willow and Nicholas Peter Willow – only with no address to be sent to. None of them, not even the teachers, knew where they were going. 'That's part of the adventure,' Carrie's mother had said, and not just to cheer them up: it was her nature to look on the bright side. If she found herself in Hell, Carrie thought now, she'd just say, 'Well, at least we'll be *warm*.'

Faith Jacques' original illustration for Chapter 2 of *Carrie's War* shows the two children, Carrie and Nick, with Miss Evans outside Samuel's grocery shop, which was to be their home during the evacuation.

Two covers from different editions of *Carrie's War* – the original 1974 Puffin cover illustration by Amy Burch, and a 1995 special Michael Joseph hardback edition, illustrated by Mark Edwards. Other covers have featured stills from a BBC television production, a photographic montage, and even a design from an American TV series.

One of the most famous children's books written about World War II is *Carrie's War*, by Nina Bawden, which was first published by Penguin Books in 1974. The story of Carrie and Nick, wartime evacuees billeted in Wales with old Mr Evans and his sister Auntie Lou, is based on events which really happened to the author, and characters whom she really met.

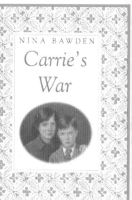

I was evacuated with my school as most older children were. We were billeted in Ipswich to begin with, and then, when Hitler invaded what our head teacher called 'the Low Countries' we were sent to Wales. We didn't know we were going to Wales, just that we were 'going west'. We were put on a train with a small suitcase each and our gas masks – which I'm glad to say I never had to use . . . When we got to Wales we trudged along a cinder path and ended up in a church hall where lots of women were waiting with tea and biscuits – and to choose the evacuees they liked the look of best. I was with my best friend which made it more fun than it would have been if I had been alone. My friend, Jean, and I had about seven billets in the years we stayed in Aberdare; our foster parents were all kind, and I think did their best for us, but we had some strange experiences. One place we stayed, the house was kept locked and bolted; when we came home from school and rang the bell it took about twenty minutes for the door to be opened. In another billet we were only allowed to go up and down the stairs once a day in case we wore out the stair-carpet. And in another, our foster father, who was a miner, came home from his shift at six in the evening and stood naked in a tin bath one side of the kitchen while his wife sluiced him down with a pail, and we did our homework at the table.

It was in its way an adventure. We saw the inside of other people's homes and families, which was very useful to me as a writer!

I hope this information is helpful. If you want more, try In My Own Time*, which has a whole chapter on the subject.*

Best wishes

A letter from
Nina Bawden

There have been many other stories written for children, about World War II. These include *When Hitler Stole Pink Rabbit* by Judith Kerr (1971), *The Machine Gunners* by Robert Westall (1975), *Goodnight Mr Tom* by Michelle Magorian (1981) and most recently *Blitzed* by Robert Swindells.

Rhyfel Sam (Sam's War) by Glenys Lloyd is a wartime story set partly in North Wales. It features a black youngster from Liverpool, who is evacuated to Anglesey for safety, as so many Liverpudlian children were.

Under Enemy Fire

Although the Blitz was centred upon London and the major English towns, Welsh cities and towns had their fair share of bombing. The three-day blitz in February 1941 left Swansea town centre in ruins. The blaze could be seen from thirty miles away.

Not a Gun was Fired

Not a gun was fired, not an airplane rose
When the bombs round the old town were popping;
Not an air-raid warden showed his nose
While the missiles were leisurely dropping;
Calmly, unhurriedly fared the Hun
From the field of his task as a vandal;
But for paralysed 'plane and silent gun –
Oh! Whom shall we blame for the scandal?

Rhyme in a local Welsh newspaper

The largest fire in Britain since 1666 – the Great Fire of London – took place in Pembroke Dock on August 19, 1940, when the oil tanks were set ablaze.

Three German planes, a Junkers 88 and two Messershmitt 109 escorts, caused tremendous damage. They met no resistance – eleven out of seventeen oil tanks were destroyed in a fire which burned for three weeks. 650 firemen fought the blaze, but 33 million gallons of oil were lost, at a time when it was vitally needed. West Wales had been caught unprepared.

Nor were people in the north of Wales safe. German fighters on missions to attack Liverpool and Birmingham often dropped their unused bombs over the countryside on their way home – and they were followed by British defending aircraft. North Wales also had lots of training areas, stop-over runways and hard-standings for transatlantic aircraft arriving from America. These were enemy targets too.

'My mother and my brother were going to feed the calves, and all of a sudden there were these two planes overhead . . . .there were bullets flying around, and my brother said, 'Where shall we go?' The plane was shot down over Waunfawr, nearer to the Snowdonia mountains . . . and the German pilot would never have escaped, so many people went out to see it come down.'
Morfudd Lewis

The coast of South Wales proved an ideal training-ground for our own fighters. There was a a 'bombing and gunnery' school at Stormy Down, a perilous hilltop airfield above Porthcawl.

'I was there in 1941, for five or six weeks . . . we used all the sand dunes and burrows around Port Talbot for ranges with targets . . . and then we fired practice bombs, ten and a half pounders into the bay . . . they just made smoke . . . they had observers in little huts who watched your errors. Then we had aircraft firing in twos . . . one with a material banner, called a drogue, streaming behind it, and the idea was that you fired your rounds, with coloured paint on them, and they made a mark on the drogue, and you knew you'd scored a hit . . .'
Wg.Cdr. John E. Tipton, DFC

Digging for Victory

As soon as the war began, people were encouraged to grow more food. The Government remembered how the food shortages in World War I had happened – when German U-boats had attacked ships carrying food, particularly corn from America – and they didn't want it

Everyone joins in the potato harvest, even the evacuees, in fields near the Preseli hills: 1942

to happen again. In 1939 Britain was still importing 60% of its food but by 1945 this had fallen to 30%. Farmers were urged first to get the 1939 harvest in, and then get ploughing, all around the clock – 'Plough Now! By Day and Night!' said the posters. Ten million acres of grassland were ploughed up, including many Welsh hillsides. Lord Anglesey ploughed up his cricket pitch, and most of his golf course. The food fight was on!

Besides needing land for cereals, such as wheat and barley, farmers needed more grass for more cows, for more milk. They needed fields for growing vegetables, especially root crops such as potatoes, turnips and carrots. Everyone knew what was happening, as cartoon characters such as Potato Pete ('I'm an Energy Man'), and Doctor Carrot ('He guards your health') appeared on posters, urging people to 'Lend a Hand on the Land' and 'Dig for Victory'. Lord Woolton, the head of the Ministry of Food, invented a vegetable pie recipe, which became a firm favourite.

and now...

PLOUGH!

With the second war harvest gathered in, not an hour should be lost in preparing for the third. So, start at once to plough the stubbles and the extra grassland — 2 million acres — that must be tilled to meet your country's needs. Remember: early ploughing means time for thorough cultivation. Good cultivation is the foe of wireworm. Time saved is food gained . . . so PLOUGH NOW.

PLOUGH for Bread for Milk for Porridge for Potatoes

Listen to the wireless Farming Talks on Thursdays—7.30 p.m. HOME SERVICE

FILL THE NATION'S LARDER

ISSUED BY THE MINISTRY OF AGRICULTURE AND FISHERIES

Increase the Yields of all your Fields

Every week the war makes heavier calls on our shipping. We must therefore produce still more food at home. This year you must make an all-out effort to produce record crops of every kind. More milk—especially for next winter. More food for the people. More feeding-stuffs for livestock. Nothing less than the maximum yield from every acre—the maximum effort from every farmer—will suffice to see us through.

YOU MUST KEEP UP THE NATION'S FOOD SUPPLY.

★ *Work by work this year will give advice to farmers—the official weekly guide to wartime farming. Watch for it regularly.*

ISSUED BY THE MINISTRY OF AGRICULTURE AND FISHERIES

Farmers were awarded a diploma when the wartime milk yield was good

Victory Churn Contest
(1944-45)

This Diploma is awarded to the Farmer & Farmworkers of Kilvrodan, Narberth in the County of Pembroke. in recognition of their loyal work for their Country in its time of need. The milk production of this Farm showed average milk sales for the whole herd of not less than two gallons per cow per day throughout the winter period.

Those who have the will to win
Cook potatoes in their skin
Knowing that the sight of peelings
Deeply hurts Lord Woolton's feeling.

Potato Pete, Potato Pete,
See him coming down the street,
Shouting his good things to eat,
'Get your potatoes from Potato Pete.'

Everyone with a garden was asked to dig up the lawn to grow vegetables, which could replace the fruit that was no longer coming by sea from other countries. Railway embankments and even the edges of football pitches became gardens. Local councils put land aside for people without gardens, and the Minister offered '10 rod-allotments' to suitable applicants. Even a window box could grow radishes, spring onions and runner beans.

Dig for Victory, Dig it now!
Feed your chickens, share a sow.
Know your onions, grow them too,
Make your garden work for you.

Families could also help the food war by keeping livestock such as chickens and rabbits, or even join together with their neighbours to set up a 'pig club'. A pig in the garage or shed would eat up any waste food, and then could be eaten itself. It seemed like a good idea, until the new family pets had to appear on the table for Sunday lunch!

HOME GROWN

'Many people kept a pig, which provided us with bacon, pork, brawn and faggots. It was illegal to accept a full bacon ration if you had a pig, so many people hid their pigs away. An inspector visited our area to check out the situation, and there is a story of an old lady taking the pig to bed with her, and hiding it under the eiderdown. Of course, the inspector would probably have been given a leg of pork or a few faggots to persuade him to keep quiet and not report the wrong-doer!'

Ann Rosser

Food and the Ration Book

On 19th September 1939, only sixteen days after war had been declared, the Ministry of Food made everyone fill in a form, giving the names and ages of the people in the house. Then ration books were sent out, and people registered with their local butcher, grocer and milkman.

A RAID ON THE FOOD CONTROLLER!

R.B.1
16

MINISTRY OF FOOD 1953-1954

SERIAL NO.
AT 423466

RATION BOOK

Surname *Paskin*   Initials *Elaine*
Address *30 Wesley Avenue*
Lyde Green
Cradley, Staffs

IF FOUND RETURN TO ANY FOOD OFFICE

F.O. CODE No.
M – D
1 – 4

Rationing started in January 1940. The first foods to be rationed were butter, sugar, bacon and ham. In March all types of meat were rationed, and tea rationing soon followed. A child under six was allowed 11 pence worth of meat a week (about 5p in today's money).

People had to change their eating habits quickly. They needed help. Marguerite Patten, a famous cookery writer, was a Food Advisor in the Ministry of Food. She remembers that her job was *'to help people make the best use of the rations available, and most of all the un-rationed food.'* Today she writes that her

If people wanted a special cake for a birthday – or to send to their fathers and husbands in the forces, then *The Stork Wartime Cookery Book* had great ideas for decorating cakes – for a soldier, a sailor or an airman. All that was needed was icing sugar, some coloured paints and plenty of imagination.

Army Cake (see pages 20 and 23)

Air Force Cake (see pages 20 and 23)

The **Stork** Wartime Cookery Book

Gypsy Tart, along with Spam Fritters, seems to be one of the happy memories of wartime school meals: it had a great appeal to children. One of the things to remember is that we could not import foods from abroad so had to depend on home-grown fruit and vegetables. I encouraged people to cook their vegetables correctly so they retained the maximum vitamins and minerals.

I hope this information is helpful.
Kindest regards,

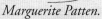

Marguerite Patten.

By 'Digging for Victory' people could grow most of the fruit and vegetables which were essential for their good health, but what if they fancied something a bit more exotic? They had to improvise.

Oranges are grown in warm countries. We can enjoy them fresh here by importing them from abroad, but this wasn't possible in the war. Oranges – and bananas, lemons and grapefruit for that matter (but not avocados: no-one had heard of them!) – were a rare treat indeed. So we had to make use of what we did have, as this recipe shows.

Simon Hickmott, *Future Foods, Rooted in the Past…*

Orange flavour whip
from a Ministry of Food pamphlet, 1945

Ingredients:	450g tinned plums
	2½ tbsp (35ml) dried milk
	3 tbsp (45ml) marmalade
Method:	Mash the plums, dried milk and marmalade. Serve in small dishes topped with marmalade or custard

Coffee too is imported over long distances and was very scarce in wartime. But some other plants taste of coffee, if prepared in the right way. Chicory is better known as a leaf vegetable, but its roasted root makes a very acceptable coffee substitute.

Gypsy Tart

Ingredients for the pastry

6 oz/175 g plain flour

pinch salt

3 oz/85g margarine

water to bind

Ingredients for the filling

1 oz/25g butter or margarine

2oz/50g sugar, preferably Demerara

1 level teaspoon golden syrup

1 large egg, whisked

¼ pint/150ml unsweetened evaporated milk

Method :

1. Sift the flour and salt, rub in the margarine then add enough water to bind. If time permits form into a neat shape, wrap and chill for 20 to 30 minutes.

2. Preheat the oven to 200ºC/400ºF, Gas Mark 6 or 180 to 190ºC with a fan oven. Roll out the pastry and line an 8inch/20cm flan tin or ring on an upturned baking tray (this makes it easier to slide the shape off the baking tray).

3. If possible chill the shape for a short time then line the pastry shape and bake blind for 15 minutes only. Remove from the oven, take out the paper or foil and immediately reduce the heat to 160º/325ºF, Gas Mark 3 or 140 to 150ºC with a fan oven.

4. While the pastry is cooking prepare the filling. Cream the butter or margarine with the sugar and syrup, add the egg and evaporated milk. Spoon into the partially baked pastry case and bake for a further 25 to 30 minutes, or until the filling is firm. Serve cold.

Dad's Army
and the Home Front

Not everyone could march off to join the forces. Some men had important work to do at home – farmers, priests, shopkeepers, doctors – and some were too old. They did, however, 'volunteer' to play their part in protecting the country from enemy attack. The Home Guard, nicknamed Dad's Army because many were too old to fight abroad, grew out of the Local Defence Volunteers (LDV for short), which also had a nickname, the 'Look, Duck and Vanish' boys. By the end of 1940 any man at home aged between 17 and 65 had to join – and volunteer for 48 hours' duty each month. Jobs included watching for the enemy, halting motorists and checking passes, and even killing pigeons, in case invading Germans used them for sending messages!

If you'd got a shotgun, like I had, being a farmer, you brought it along . . . there was talk about using hay-forks and such for drill, but we never did that . . . .

After a while we had Lee Enfield rifles . . . they were dreadful old things, and we'd be practising with rifles every Sunday morning up at our Headquarters on the Golf Course . . . And then we had American rifles, they came from the First World War, twenty in a wooden box, covered with vaseline, or petroleum jelly you'd say . . . all our overalls got dirty getting them free of grease.

And then there was bayonet practice . . . you had to sort out the manoeuvres, 1,2,3,4, . . . a bag was filled with hay and suspended off the branch of a tree or something, in the Golf Club car park, and then you approached it . . . in, twist, pull, back, ooofh! We didn't really like that; we realised the Germans would be doing that practice as well.

John Francis

In the years when our Country was in mortal danger

HENRY ADAMS

who served 12 July 1940 – 31 December 1944 gave generously of his time and powers to make himself ready for her defence by force of arms and with his life if need be.

George R.I.

THE HOME GUARD

Even before September 1939 people were getting ready for war, as the ARP (Air Raid Precautions) cigarette cards from 1938 show. People were advised on which room to use as a refuge room, and how to equip it.

'Having rendered it gas-proof . . . you should furnish it with the following articles: Table and chairs. Gum and paper for sealing windows and cracks. Tinned food and a tin to contain bread . . . Books, writing materials, cards etc. to pass the time with . . . Plenty of water in jugs for drinking, washing, fire-fighting etc. Chamber pots, toilet paper, disinfectant . . .'

'Aunty Lil had a long thin room off the downstairs hall, with bunk beds in . . . to a small child it seemed very safe and cosy.'

Once the war started, people with gardens were issued with air-raid shelters, called Anderson Shelters, named after the Home Secretary Sir John Anderson. They looked like tunnels made of corrugated sheets, and had to be half-buried about a metre below ground. Some people put soil on the roof and grew vegetables on it. After the war people uncovered the Anderson shelters and used them as garden sheds – or Wendy houses!

This leaflet was distributed across North Wales, telling people what to do if German troops landed – and how to do it. The information, in both English and Welsh, made sure that the readers understood that the Germans 'will be driven out by our Navy, our Army and our Air Force' and that they needed to be ready to assist. 'You must not be taken by surprise,' says the leaflet.

Air Raid Wardens were specially trained to advise their neighbours and fellow citizens on what to do if there were bomb attacks, and to act as reporting agents of any bomb damage. They wore special helmets, and were entitled to wear an ARP badge,

'I was brought up in Llansamlet which was situated between Llandarcy oil refinery and Swansea, which were targets for the German bombing raids. So the ARP was an important defence mechanism in my home area. My father was the head warden in our village, and he and all the other wardens wore helmets with W on the front. His name was Wendal, and I remember being confused because the man next door was called Fred – and he didn't have a helmet with F on it.'
Ann Rosser

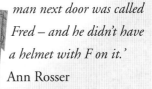

Working Women

Not everyone could go off to war and fight – but with many men away in the Armed Forces, women and girls were asked to play their part on the war effort. The Women's Land Army played a vital part in the farming life of Britain in the war years. The girls learned many skills, including thatching, hedging and ditching, tractor driving – and even chopping down trees.

Girls from Usk enjoying a break from forestry work at The Graig. The Women's Timber Corp was formed in 1942. The girls learned to wield a 7lb-axe, and cut down trees for fencing posts, pit props and telegraph poles.

We stayed in the Land Army Hostel in Raglan, and we went out from there daily; we weren't attached to any one farm. We did milking by hand, poultry farming and horticulture, and a bit of forestry in Monmouth, at The Graig, Rocklands . . . oh, and ploughing, but we didn't have to do the pigs. We had to drive the prisoners of war to work, the Germans and Italians. I think the worst job was topping and tailing swedes on a frosty morning, and then taking them down to Usk station where the trains were standing ready to take them away . . . we had to work as hard as any man.

Margaret Williams and Beryl Fouweather trained at Usk Institute of Agriculture. They have been friends ever since that time in the Women's Land Army. Margaret still has her heavy brown shoes and her badge which she proudly wore on her tie.

The women were guaranteed work for a year, with one week's holiday with pay, and were allowed to be off duty on Saturday and Sunday evenings. They were issued with a standard uniform, a pair of brown corduroy breeches, a beige skirt, a green jumper and a khaki overcoat. Also a brown hat, thick stockings, Wellingtons, heavy brown shoes, and two pairs of boots.

A rare World War II 'Barribal' postcard celebrates the Land Army girls. One of a series of 'pin-ups' which tried to make wartime occupations for women seem glamorous!

I love the Farmers

We had 10 shillings a week rising to twelve and six after a year, plus our keep and our uniform. The food wasn't too special – when we went to the fields we had cabbage sandwiches, and the POWs (prisoners of war) had bacon, under the Geneva convention – but we were healthy, we had very little illness.

And we had lots of fun. We had ENSA concerts, and we used to go down to Clytha Hall for dances when the army were billeted there – we went there on our bikes, in the dark, in our thick khaki socks and knee breeches . . . I had a rat put down my back once . . . I was strung up on a pulley, two men got my belt and turned me upside down! I was in bed for two days . . . they'd shoved mice down my trousers. Another time we went to London to be a guard of honour at a wedding . . . how we got those pitchforks up there on the train I don't know.
Beryl Fouweather, and Margaret Williams

Despite all the fun and games, the Women's Land Army – whose volunteers ranged from 13 to 82 years of age – played a vital part in 'Lending a Hand on the Land'.

Other women joined special parts of the Armed Service. The WAAF (Women's Auxiliary Air Force) had 1700 members at the outbreak of war. By 1945 this number had risen to 180,000. There were 15 different types of duty – including catering, transport, telephony and Intelligence and Security.

The WRNS, or Women's Royal Naval Service had been created in World War I, so that women could do on-shore jobs and 'Free a Man for Sea Service'. It was quickly reformed in 1939 and by 1944 there were 74,000 women doing all kinds of jobs. Many helped to run the navy's activities on shore, and thousands of others served overseas.

The badges of Leading WREN writer Janet Francis. She was a clerical worker, responsible for the smooth running of her camp.

Families at War

Being a war baby
Wasn't much fun,
I only saw my Daddy once
Before I was one,
And then it was only
For a night and a day,
He was off to Russian waters
Chasing submarines away.

Being a war baby
Was just hard luck,
Too much bottled orange juice
And Virol syrup, Yuck!
Hardly any chocolate
Or minty humbugs –
Had to make do with
Granny's sweet-lipped hugs.

Being a war baby
Was quite a scary thing,
Lying in my cot
With home-made blankets to my chin.
It was always black-out
Through the long dark night,
Mustn't let the Germans see
One chink of light,

Being a war baby
Is now such good news,
I'm quite a celebrity
Visiting schools,
Answering the questions
That children want to know –
What babies did in wartime:
I tell them so!

Although family life was different in the war years – and for some it would never be the same again – many events remained the same: births, marriages and even deaths.

Babies born in the war didn't see their fathers very often; fathers saw little of their children. Family snapshots became important links, and were precious reminders of normal family back home. When rationing came, babies had special foods and medicines to keep them healthy. Wartime posters reminded mothers not to 'forget baby's cod liver oil and orange juice'.

'One of my earliest memories is of being carried to the sound of the siren (an eerie sounding hooter which warned of an air raid) to the shelter under the house. I was zipped up in a blue 'siren suit' which I loved. I never understood why everyone looked so happy when the "all clear" hooter went . . . because I never wanted to go back to bed!' – Ann Rosser

With boyfriends and girlfriends about to be separated, there was a rush for young people to get married, either before the men were called up for service, or when they were on leave. Special passes were needed, as the bridegrooms applied for 'compassionate leave'. Clothing coupons were gathered together for that all-important dress. Sometimes it was made from the white silk of parachutes.

There were sad times as well as happy times in most wartime families. Everyone dreaded the business-like 'knock on the door' by the police, or the telegram boy on his bicycle, bringing a letter from the Ministry of War.

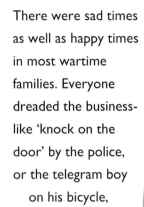

Flight-Sergeant Edwin Shaw's aircraft was reported missing over France on 15 April, 1943. This letter informs his father of his death. His grave is in a tiny wooded cemetery in central France. It is soldiers like him whom we remember on Remembrance Day, on November 11th every year.

Stamped 28th August 1941, this request form gives Tom Paskin leave to travel from Portsmouth to Birmingham, to marry his sweetheart from teenage days, Kathleen Homer. Notice that the number of days has been reduced in pencil – from Friday till Monday, not Wednesday!

REQUEST FORM.

Ship's Book No. 2638   Mess E.2.8.
Watch BLUE   Duty
Name in full THOMAS PASKIN
Rating A/E (mw)   Official No. FX81425
Non-Sub. Rating   Badges
"T," "G" or "U.A." T.

REQUEST : For Leave out of watch with Green Watch, Reason, For purpose of getting married. From 12 noon Fri till first train Wed morning, with warrant. Travelling from Portsmouth to Birmingham, New St. Station

ADDRESS WHILST ON LEAVE:
17 Mill St.
Bradley

Treasure in the Mountains

At the beginning of the war 6000 famous pictures and paintings were moved out of London for safety from the air-raids. They were brought by rail to Bangor and Aberystwyth, but then it was decided that they weren't even safe in the buildings there, especially when the Germans bombers targeted Liverpool.

Officials from the National Gallery in London decided the pictures needed to be safe underground, and they chose Manod slate quarry, near Ffestiniog, as the best place. The paintings would have a 65-metre thick roof to keep them safe from aerial bombing! The quarry chambers were fitted with special fans to keep the pictures dry and warm at 65° F.

The pictures were then moved on lorries to the treasure store. The road to the quarry entrance was four miles long. It was a winding narrow lane, and the lorries couldn't pass one another, so the drivers needed a very careful timetable. The entrance itself had to be widened so that the lorries could be driven inside and the gates closed before the valuable paintings were unloaded.

The safety precautions turned out to be a good idea, because the National Gallery in London was bombed in 1940. Many pictures would have been destroyed if they had not been moved to safety.

Art Treasures

Into the secret silence of Manod
quarry they deposited like Hamelin's children

the National's collection of air-conditioned art,
safeguarded for posterity inside a Welsh cavern

to escape for five years
the blitz of a city's acid heart.

Impressionism in central Gwynedd,
Rembrandt next to Ffestiniog's slate,

sculpted to remember, not to be erased,
the palettes of durable colour,

an exact style entering the darkness
brightening a craggy mouth in Wales.

Byron Beynon

Only two large paintings caused trouble on the journey. One was of Charles I on horseback by Van Dyck. It was so large that the road under the Ffestiniog Railway arch had to be dug out by nearly a metre, so the lorry, with its precious cargo, could get under the bridge.

A painting being loaded into an LMS (London, Scottish, Midland) Railway lorry, at University College, Bangor. Notice the white painted mudguards, to help other motorists see the lorry in the blackouts.

On the Coupons

Fashions and Furniture

In the early years of the war all sorts of goods, besides food, became difficult to buy – toys, clothes, saucepans and furniture were all in short supply.

Fashion was put 'on the ration' in June 1941, and people needed coupons to buy most clothing. Everyone had a clothing coupons book, and lists appeared which told you how many coupons you needed. Girls' pyjamas needed six coupons, and boys' shoes three coupons, as well as money for the cost of the goods, of course. A new Utility range of fashion was introduced in 1942 under the Civilian Clothing Order, with 34 designs. The rules were: no frills, no more than 3 buttons, and shorter skirts. The makers of these garments had to sew a special label inside them – CC41. (Civilian Clothing 1941).

Solve the Coupon Problem with the Coat Illustrated !

You'll find full value for your coupons and your money in this full-length coat in MOKKASKIN which looks like real Persian Lamb. You'll enjoy wearing this coat this year, and next year too, as it will always be fashionable and useful. In Black only. Sizes : S.W., W., W.X. and O.S.

Price 11 GNS.

IMPORTANT NOTICE!

Revised Shopping Hours.

Monday to Wednesday	... ...	5.30 p.m.
Thursday	... ...	1.0 p.m.
Friday and Saturday	... ...	5.30 p.m.

Lewis Lewis

(THE DRAPERS)

Lewis Lewis (Swansea) Ltd., 27-29, High Street, Swansea. Tel.: 2044.

Each ration book contained 66 coupons – a year's supply. To buy this MOKKASKIN coat from Lewis Lewis the Drapers in Swansea you would probably need to use 15 coupons – as well as paying 11 guineas in cash (£10.55p).

In 1942 a scheme was introduced to produce Utility furniture. Quality designers were invited to submit ideas for plain furniture which would be economical to make – and not use too much fine timber. Backs of wardrobes and bottoms of drawers would be made of hardboard. 20 designs were approved, and were made in 700 factories across Britain. The first Utility furniture, available on coupons, was in the stores in early 1943. Not everyone was impressed – the papers called it 'shoddy and second rate'!

'I was very excited to have my own bedroom furniture – a single wardrobe and a 'tall boy' with cupboards in the top, and drawers in the bottom. The pieces had imitation brass handles like little ping-pong balls, and were very well polished . . . but they always smelled of moth balls or something. The furniture was supposed to be temporary, like prefab houses, but we were still using it in the 1980s.'

Everybody had to 'make do and mend', as this Board of Trade booklet from 1943 suggests. Mrs Sew and Sew became a popular advertising figure in magazines and at the cinema. Women who were good at sewing were encouraged to 'turn out and renovate' and even change men's suits into garments for themselves! Anyone who could design a dress, cut out a paper pattern, and make something new and stylish from old material was the envy of her neighbours. Mothers might also be asked to 'unpick it and knit it again' to give children's old jumpers and baby clothes a new life.

Home Thoughts
from Abroad

Soldiers were not only fighting across the Channel in France and Belgium – many were posted to Italy, and others to North Africa. Their families back home were always anxious for news and letters, particularly at Christmas time. Service men were issued with special cards. Notice the special 'PASSED BY CENSOR' stamp in the top corner. The writers had to be careful what they wrote – in case the Germans captured the post, and found out where the British troops were.

Joe Chamberlain sent 'hearty greetings oer land sea and air' to his wife in Cathays, Cardiff.

Sydney Griffiths, (on the left) wished his wife Sally a 'happy and victorious New Year' in Pontrhydyfen, Port Talbot. Sydney was something of a poet – he always wrote a verse to his 'darling sweetheart' on the back of his cards. On this 1943 card from the Eighth Army in North Africa is a poem called 'I Think of You'. It ends with these lines:

'I miss you in the evening most, the time we held so dear
When twilight softly gathers and the dusk is drawing near
And though my hands are busy, yet my heart is lonely still
And there's a voice of comradeship that only you can fill.'

Yours Ever Lovingly
Syd xxxxxxxxx
xxxxxxxxx

Search and Find

It was hot on the tank landing craft – boiling hot and very boring. My father was on his way back from Italy to rejoin his tank unit in the 23rd Armoured Brigade. After receiving a bullet wound to his leg, he'd been invalided out across the Mediterranean to be treated in a North African hospital.

Now he was better and on that tank landing craft and looking for something to do. For days he joined in card games, mainly pontoon. But, as he afterwards used to say, you cannot live on pontoon. Something to remember for the future was that the padre on board was the brother of Monty, the great war general. But that didn't make any difference to the heat and boredom of the days. My father was desperate – desperate for something to read. Reading was what he loved to do, one reason why he'd become an English teacher, and now he began to search. 'Every hole and corner', he later recorded, 'every crack and cranny of that tank landing craft, was probed and searched and emptied. Hope wore out.'

He came to the last bunker. It had a ring-pull lid. He lifted the ring and underneath saw a pile of dirty, oily sacking. Though he never knew quite why, he lifted the sacking.

And underneath were three books. One he would quickly forget; it was a nonentity. Another turned out to be a very good novel, aptly entitled The Road Back. The third was by Charles Dickens, one of his favourite writers, and it was one of the great finds of his life. He read it and re-read it and carried it about in his kitbag until he got home to Pembrokeshire at the end of the war. In the circumstances it couldn't have been better named. It was Great Expectations.

Note: My father, David James, was in the 50th Tank Unit of the 23rd Armoured Brigade. Before being called up he was English master at Milford Central School and he returned to that job at the end of the war.

Mary Medlicott, storyteller

Books, Toys

and Entertainment

During the war, there weren't many new toys. Many of the best metal toys – cars and trains – had been made in Germany, and of course these weren't available. Bakelite aeroplanes and tanks, lead soldiers and dolls in uniforms were popular for acting out battles. If you were lucky enough to a have a Bayko No 5 building set, the pre-war answer to Lego, you could also build your own barracks, to train your model army.

There were always books to buy, although use of paper was restricted, and books had to be printed on government-approved paper. Enid Blyton's first Famous Five adventure, called *Five on a Treasure Island* was published in 1942.

Captain Biggles was the most popular wartime hero. The first stories about him, published from 1932 onwards, were set in World War I.

Biggles books are still popular today. He was one of the stars of the 1994 Royal Mail stamps, featuring favourite characters from children's literature.

Worrals hesitated, not quite sure what to do next.

152

Clearly, it was not the moment to disturb the woman.

153

In *Worrals Goes East* (1944) the two heroines, surviving murder attempts involving snakes in beds and poisoned chocolates, reach a secret enemy outpost in the Arabian desert, and uncover a secret German printing press, operated by the mysterious Fraulein Hylda.

With girl readers in mind, the War Ministry persuaded his creator, Captain W E Johns, to invent a new heroine to aid recruitment to the Women's Auxiliary Air Force. So 'Worralls of the WAAF' was born, and Flight Officer Joan Worralson and her side-kick F.O. Betty 'Frecks' Lovell got into all sorts of wartime scrapes, ferrying machines to the fighting squadrons, attacking Nazi camel trains and generally confusing the Germans. WE Johns also created a soldier hero, 'Gimlet', King of the Commandos, who appeared in two wartime novels for young people.

The cinema was also very popular in wartime Britain. Everybody went to the 'flicks' and saw Walt Disney cartoons which are still favourites with children today. *Snow White and the Seven Dwarfs*, first issued in 1937, was re-released in 1944, and *Pinocchio* (1940), *Fantasia* (1940) and *Bambi* (1942) helped people to escape from the worries of life at home.

Just like today, you could buy souvenirs at the ticket office – or send postcards to your friends. These cards were posted in Glasgow in April 1943.

FROM THE WALT DISNEY FILM "PINOCCHIO"

"THIS CALLS FOR A CELEBRATION! SO THEY ALL MADE FRIENDS OF PINOCCHIO"

WALT DISNEY'S *Snow White and the Seven Dwarfs*

"SO THE LITTLE PRINCESS KNEW AT LAST THE MIRACLE OF DREAMS COME TRUE."

Days at School

The beginning of the war upset school life. Gas mask practice, air-raid sirens and the arrival of evacuees meant that everything was topsy-turvy for a little while, but gradually life settled into the old routine. Teachers were sometimes absent, if there had been bombing the previous night in their home town or village, and of course men teachers went off to fight, and older people were brought out of retirement to fill the gaps. Sometimes the serving teachers came back to describe their exciting lives on Commando raids.

Children became involved in the 'War Effort', particularly with the National Savings Movement. Every class in every school had a savings target to meet. You weren't giving away your money, you were lending it. Just as today, there were poster competitions – for 'War Weapons Week', or 'National Warship Week', and this meant a trip to the local town hall to view the exhibition of entries.

> *1944*
> *May 15th:*
> *'Salute the Soldiers' Week, under the National Savings Movement commenced today. The target set for our school is £400.*
>
> *May 22nd:*
> *Total collected from all classes for SSW amounted to £1032.0.0*

There was sometimes the chance of an afternoon out of school to see a propaganda film, perhaps about saving useful waste – paper, jam jars, rags and bones, and even saucepans. 2000 aluminium saucepans make one aeroplane – or so they said!

A wartime seed catalogue from Suttons, and a Commemorative Seed Packet 1945-1995, which contained 4 varieties of common wartime vegetables – including CARROT Sutton's Favourite, and RADISH Scarlet Globe.

And of course there was the school garden to tend, and the chance to 'Dig for Victory'. Seed potatoes were ordered from the CWS (Cooperative Wholesale Society), seed catalogues were examined, and varieties of vegetables chosen. In many areas senior pupils were given official 'time off' to help local farmers pick their potatoes, or plant them, depending on the time of year. In rural areas whole schools closed to help with the haymaking and agricultural work.

8th June, 1946

To-day, as we celebrate victory, I send this personal message to you and all other boys and girls at school. For you have shared in the hardships and dangers of a total war and you have shared no less in the triumph of the Allied Nations.

I know you will always feel proud to belong to a country which was capable of such supreme effort; proud, too, of parents and elder brothers and sisters who by their courage, endurance and enterprise brought victory. May these qualities be yours as you grow up and join in the common effort to establish among the nations of the world unity and peace.

George R.I.

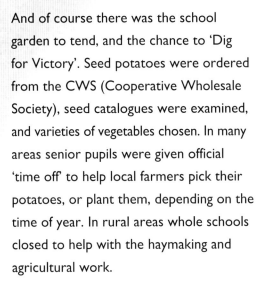

1942

Jan 28th:
short sessions, to enable Seniors
to see a film re School Gardening

Feb 20th:
School Gardening film at Fenton.
Top class boys attended at 3.00pm
with Mr Morgan in charge.

Envelope full of Gardening slogans
sent to the Agricultural Organiser,
County Office, to be entered
for the competition.

March 26th:
W Dicken, Std IV awarded prize
in slogan competition by Pembrokeshire
Agricultural Committee, for
'DIG IN TO SAVE FORKING OUT'

School Log Book: Haverfordwest VC School

Sometimes there were extra holidays. On September 3rd each year there was a special assembly, usually taken by the local minister, for the National Day of Prayer and Thanksgiving on the anniversary of the outbreak of war. Then the whole school would have the rest of the day off. And, of course, at the end of the war there were two days holiday, to celebrate VE Day. A while later, there came a letter from King George himself, thanking school-children for their part in the Victory.

Victory Parade

On May 8th 1945 the Germans surrendered. The war was over. People danced in the streets and lit bonfires in the parks. Winston Churchill, the prime minister, and King George VI spoke to everyone on the radio. There were two days of national holiday – V Day and V Day Plus One. These days celebrated the Victory in Europe.

Street parties were quickly arranged. New recipes appeared, like Victory Sponge, as everyone went wild with their rations and prepared to enjoy themselves. It was party time in Wales, as villages and towns welcomed home their loved ones.

'Welcome Home Social: there was a large gathering at the schoolroom on Friday evening to give a welcome home to Pte Martin Jones . . . who is home after three years of active service in north Africa and Italy . . . The ladies are to be heartily congratulated on the splendid manner in which refreshments were given and served. The musical part of the programme opened with the Welsh National anthem, the solo part being taken by Miss Madge Davies . . . The usual gift of £1 was presented to Pte M Jones by the grand old lady of the parish, Mrs Hetty Williams, Belmont, who is in her 94th year. Congratulatory speeches were delivered by the Vicar . . .'

News clipping of Llawhaden celebrations

VJ Day came on 15th August, when the war in Japan was over. There were more celebrations, more Thanksgiving Services, more speeches – and more street parties!

When the Victory parades were on we were invited with the RAF to parade through Pontypool, Newport and Blaenavon, in our uniforms, and we were well-received, fair play!
- Beryl Fouweather, Women's Land Army

Celebrations at Twthill, Caernarfon

Victory Celebrations

Flags fluttering as if even the breeze is happy,
Bunting stretched across the street,
A great trestle table with white cloth gleaming,
Groaning with delicious food – oh, what a treat!

Sun shining down, I think the war is over,
Everyone's making so much noise,
*Ei gwrol ryfelwyr, gwladgarwyr tra mad * –*
We're singing for our returning soldier boys.

Bright blue the sky, I feel it's like a mirror,
Reflecting our memories and wartime tales,
*Tros ryddid collasant eu gwaed ***
But some will never come home to Wales.

Francesca Kay

* Its warring defenders so gallant and bold
** For freedom their life's blood they gave

British Library Cataloguing in Publication Data
Stephens, Christopher S.
A wartime scrapbook
1. World War, 1939-1945 – Social aspects – Wales – Juvenile literature
2. World War, 1939-1945 – Wales – Juvenile literature 3. Family – Wales – History – 20th century – Juvenile literature
I. Title
940.5'31'09429

First publication 2004

ISBN 1 84323 390 8 (hardback)   ISBN 1 84323 285 5 (softback)

Printed in Wales at Gomer Press, Llandysul, Ceredigion.

Original illustrations

Endpapers: Elizabeth Dyer; Ration queue (p.3): Fran Evans
Evacuee twins (p.5): Maggy Roberts; Pembroke Dock fire (p.8-9): Brett Breckon
Chicory (p.11): Simon Hickmott; Wren (p.17): Suzanne Carpenter
Manod quarry (p.20) and David James (p.25): Graham Howells
Utility furniture (p.23): Edmund Stephens.

Acknowledgements

The author and publishers gratefully acknowledge the generosity of the following, who have loaned
material or given permission for material to be reproduced in this book:
Glenys Adams; Jano Bevan; Phil Carradice; Marian Davies; Pip Jones; the Ledger family; Elaine Lidgate; Bethan Mair; Joan Peake;
Stephanie and Richard Tilley; Janet Tomey; Elaine Walker; Margaret Williams and Beryl Fouweather, former Land Army girls; Reg Chambers Jones
for illustrations from Bless 'Em All, Bridge Books, 1995, and for specific illustrations, Mr Aled Jones (p.4, 15) and Mrs Doris Rogers (p.31);
Haverfordwest V.C. School; Narberth Museum Ltd; Pembrokeshire Museum Services; West Glamorgan Archive Service (p.8);
Peter Maurice Music Co. Ltd for sheet music, 'Victory Parade' (p.30); Royal Doulton plc (figures, p.4); Suttons Consumer Products Ltd (p.11, 28);
National Gallery Company Ltd for 'Equestrian Portrait of Charles I' by Van Dyck © National Gallery, London and also Manod Quarry
photographs (p.21); Hodder Headline for pages from Worrals Goes East by W.E. Johns, Hodder and Stoughton, 1944; Penguin Books Ltd for an extract
from Carrie's War by Nina Bawden (Puffin, 1974) copyright © Nina Bawden 1973, and the illustration, © copyright Faith Jaques (p.6);
Penguin Books Ltd also for cover illustrations by Amy Burch and Mark Edwards (p.6). The presentation card which accompanied
the Biggles stamps (p.26) is reproduced by kind permission of Royal Mail plc.

It has not been possible to trace the owner of copyright in every case. The publishers apologise for
any ommission and invite copyright owners to contact them so that any oversight can be remedied for re-printing.